PAST LIVES, PRESENT KARMA

WORKBOOK

by

BETTYE B. BINDER

REINCARNATION BOOKS/TAPES

P.O. BOX 7781

CULVER CITY, CA 90233-7781

Phone: (310) 397-5757

BIOGRAPHY OF THE AUTHOR

BETTYE B. BINDER

Bettye B. Binder is a teacher of Reincarnation and Metaphysics, author and
past life regression counselor, who has
done more than 3000 past life regression
and taught over 13,000 people.

She earned a BA from Barnard College
(1960) and an MA from Columbia University
Graduate School (1962) in New York City
majoring in political science and public
administration. For 20 years she worked
in politics, government service, consumer
organizations, market research, and
various writing positions. However,
spontaneous memories of her past life as
an American Indian female living in the
Southwestern United States in the 1700's
led her to change careers in 1980.

She teaches classes using her books as
textbooks and presents workshops at Whole
Life Expo in Los Angeles and other cities.
She has been a member of the Association
for Past Life Research and Therapies
(APRT) since 1981. In 1991, she was
elected First Vice President.

BETTYE HAS WRITTEN AND PUBLISHED
FOUR BOOKS:

PAST LIFE REGRESSION GUIDEBOOK
PAST LIVES, PRESENT KARMA WORKBOOK
MEDITATIVE AND PAST LIFE JOURNAL
**FINDING YOUR LIFE'S PURPOSE THROUGH
 ASTROLOGY WORKBOOK**, co-authored with
 astrologer, Mark Vito.

All 4 were published by her company,
Reincarnation Books/Tapes.
She has also written a fifth book,
WHAT WERE YOU IN YOUR PAST LIFE?
published by Globe Communications,
Inc., 1993.

BETTYE BINDER HAS CREATED SIX
SPOKEN AUDIO VOLUMES OF HER CLASSES

PAST LIFE REGRESSION
PAST LIVES, PRESENT KARMA
MEDITATIVE AND PAST LIFE JOURNAL
FINDING YOUR LIFE'S PURPOSE THROUGH
 ASTROLOGY
PSYCHIC PHENOMEN OF REINCARNATION
and
LIFE, DEATH AND REINCARNATION: THE
 SOUL'S CHOICES

Bettye also appeared on the Fox
Broadcasting tv show, **SIGHTINGS**,
about past life regression on
July 17, 1992.

You can buy Bettye's books and tapes
from New Age bookstores or from her
company, REINCARNATION BOOKS/TAPES,
P.O. Box 7781, Culver City, CA 90233-
7781. Phone: (310) 397-5757.

ACKNOWLEDGEMENTS

PAST LIVES, PRESENT KARMA WORKBOOK combines my research from several sources in
addition to my own teaching experience.

First, I acknowledge Dr. Loy Young, my
teacher in past life regression and co-
author of Robert and Loy Young and Lucia
Capacchione, REINCARNATION HANDBOOK, TECH-
NIQUE OF PAST LIFE REGRESSION (Los Angeles,
CA: Reincarnation Research and Education
Foundation, 1980), which is now out of
print. As a result of studying with her
in the spring of 1980, I began my professional work as a counselor and teacher of
metaphysics. When Loy moved to Hawaii in
the summer of 1980, I organized Spiritual
Awareness Center in Los Angeles, recently
dissolved. I thank Loy for her encourage-
ment of my work.

Since 1980, I have performed more than
3000 past life regressions and taught
classes to more than 13,000 students. As
I refined my techniques, I have read many
authors in this field. One in particular
influenced me a lot. He is Torkom Saraydarian, the author of THE SCIENCE OF
BECOMING ONESELF, THE FLAME OF BEAUTY,
CULTURE, LOVE, JOY and COSMOS IN MAN,
published by the Aquarian Education
Group in Agoura, California. I consider
Torkom a great theoretician and inter-
preter of the works of Alice Bailey.

I also acknowledge Lucia Capacchione,
THE CREATIVE JOURNAL, THE ART OF FIND-
ING YOURSELF (Chicago, Il: Swallow
Press, 1979). It is Lucia's notion that

our physical, emotional and mental sub-
personalities or elementals communicate
with us when we write and draw with both
hands in a journal. My expansion of
Lucia's valuable work was inspired
directly by my own dreams, journal and
meditative experiences starting in 1981.
I have now separated this material into
a new book, <u>MEDITATIVE AND PAST LIFE
JOURNAL</u>.

I also want to thank Steven Halpern
whose musical compositions, especially
<u>SPECTRUM SUITE</u>, I have used frequently
in my meditative class work. His music
has added a special quality to journal
and regression exercises in particular.

BETTYE B. BINDER
January 1986

(Revised September 1992)

INTRODUCTION

This is a practical guide to personal
and spiritual growth. It is for anyone
interested in understanding and apply-
ing knowledge of metaphysics and reincarnation to improve life today and in
the future. The techniques I outline
here promote problem-solving in the
present and also help identify karmic
patterns brought into this lifetime
from past lives.

Unresolved problems from previous existence often impinge on the present, perhaps without our consciously knowing it.
As we study present karmic patterns and
examine the past lives from which they
came, we open the way to understanding
the Soul's reasons for incarnating as
this personality in this lifetime. In so
doing, we experience the significance of
our life's lessons, no matter how hard
they may have been. This creates a new
and more positive direction for our
future.

As negative patterns are removed, we
begin to make changes in the now. This
is what is meant by "creating your own
positive Karma".

Karma is sometimes mislabeled as punishment for misdeeds in past lives.
Karma is not punishment. It is the Law
of Cause and Effect. Otherwise stated,
for every action, there is a reaction.
Negative Karma is the result of unresolved issues from the past. Positive
Karma represents their resolution.

Positive Karma often boils down to learning three basic lessons of human relations:

1. Prejudice is replaced by tolerance as you realize you have been a member of both sexes, all races, creeds, religions and nationalities in many other lifetimes.

2. Self-responsibility substitutes for victim scripts when you learn to own and express your feelings and take charge of the conduct of your own life. This is what allows the true Self to shine.

3. Self-esteem is strengthened in daily life and fear of the unknown diminishes as you find your true personal identity and spiritual Purpose.

Mastering your Karmic lessons paves the way for you to fulfill your Dharma, i.e. the Soul's spirtual purpose for being here. Learning your Karmic lessons is what this WORKBOOK is all about.

The exercises in this WORKBOOK are intended to help you solve problems here and now and open the channel to intuitive communication about your past lives.

I have designed this material to be used, over and over, again. This is why I have outlined it in simple how-to-do-it steps with a minimum of metaphysical theory. I have taught it to hundreds of people who have found it of practical use in their daily lives. You can do these exercises by yourself or with a group of friends or family members.

At the same time, if you continue to find yourself blocked or frustrated after you have done these exercises, you may want to seek the assistance of a reputable therapist or other counselor. There is nothing wrong with saying "I can't do it alone". Besides, doing these exercises may well have prepared you to seek therapy for a problem that had previously had no name.

Finally, this WORKBOOK is intended as preparation for the serious student of past life regression. The exercises here help identify problems which began in past lives and are impinging upon this lifetime. After completing this WORKBOOK you may want to read my PAST LIFE REGRESSION GUIDEBOOK. It is designed to explain the techniques by which past life regression can help resolve karmic challenges carried over from past lives.

Even the advanced student of metaphysics is urged to start with this WORKBOOK, first. It will help you better understand what karmic lessons to examine in past life regression at a later date.

TABLE OF CONTENTS

CHAPTER ONE

PREPARATION EXERCISES

The first step in doing the exercises in
this WORKBOOK is to identify the characteristics of memory and separate memory
from imagination. The purpose of doing
this first is that every exercise in this
WORKBOOK depends on understanding real
karmic issues and real memory. This dis-
tinction is especially important when
reviewing past life memory because of the
common tendency to discount it as fantasy.

In Chapter One you do a series of exercises whose goal is to define how you
perceive real memory in this lifetime.
The most important facts with which to
start are: everybody is different and
there are no right and wrong answers.
Some people are visual. Some people are
not. Some people have strong emotions and
know something is real because of their
emotional reactions. Some people perceive
through all five physical senses but not
always the same sense in each memory.
People who are highly visual often get
information more than one way. They may
be very emotional, too. However, people
who do not see anything during these
exercises often discount their validity.
These people often have a strong sense of
mental knowing of what is real. They need
to learn to trust that knowing. It is
their channel. Identifying your own personal pattern of memory in this chapter
will make the exercises in Chapters Two
and Three easier to do.

A common doubt about the validity of
Reincarnation is whether it is "make,
believe" or not. Reincarnation in the
West suffers from the fantasy of many
people who believe they were a famous
person like Napoleon in a past life.
Famous people are often surrounded by
hundreds or thousands of non-famous
people. Look how many people were at the
Battle of Waterloo! By doing the exercises in this chapter, you can determine
whose body you occupy in a memory. For
example, did you see Napoleon <u>over</u>
<u>there</u> on his horse or are you inside
his body looking at everybody else? By
repeating the exercises in this chapter,
over and over, you can counter your own
doubts with assurance. If you can see
Napoleon over there you are not inside
his body. If you can feel his emotions
in his body, not just mentally surmise
how he is feeling, then you were he.
When doubts arise, return to Chapter
One and repeat the exercises for sepa-
rating memory from imagination. Personal experience will tell you what
is real and what is fantasy.

EXERCISE I: DIFFERENCES BETWEEN MEMORY AND IMAGINATION

Typically memory differs from imagination in four basic ways. Here are the most typical differences that have shown up among students in my classes.

	MEMORY	IMAGINATION
a. Sequence:	Past events pop in clearly defined. There are no decisions to make. No effort is required to remember real events. The only exception is a trauma which in self-defense you may block out.	The sequence of events is open to change at will. Decisions are necessary to construct events and it takes effort to keep them in sequence. When you stop con-centrating on an event, it usually fades.
b. Emotions:	Memory may have strong emotional content. Even "unemotional" people or people who fabricate emotions for a living e.g.	Imagination has little or no emotional content. Manu-factured feel-ings lack the staying power of spontane-ously felt emotion. The

actors/ actresses experience emotion as having depth. Fabricated emotion does not.

exception is a depressed person who, when imagining something humorous, may feel the reality of the humor having more depth than their own feelings.

c. Recall:

Remembered events are always available for recall and are always the same. You cannot change the detail of real memory at will. You may get more detail or other details the longer you concentrate on recalling an event.

The detail of imaginary events can be changed at will. The more changes you make, the more you realize you made up the details.

d. Five Senses: Memory is often felt through experiences and sense impressions eg vivid color, memorable sounds, noticeable tastes or smells, and an ability to feel texture of familiar objects when not physically present. Imaginary events may be perceived visually but the picture is unclear or fades. Other physical senses are absent. For example, you may hear a sound when it is suggested to you, but you don't hear it spontaneously.

Emotional, visual and other physical reactions to memory are the most common ways memory is perceived. These factors validate the reality of here and now experiences in this lifetime. This lifetime memories are ordinarily perceived in the same way past life memories are.

Often, the way you perceive memory also gives hints about your astrological chart, and not just your sun sign, but also the predominance of planets in the four elements of the zodiac. Here are the correlations I have noted most often in performing past life regressions, doing work in the past life journal and reading astrological charts.

Fire Signs usually perceive through mental knowing (Leo, Aries, Sagittarius)
Air Signs usually perceive through visual seeing (Libra, Aquarius, Gemini)
Earth Signs usually perceive through the five physical senses (Taurus, Virgo, Capricorn)
Water Signs usually perceive through feeling emotionally (Pisces, Scorpio, Cancer).

Practice Exercise #1: Memory vs Imagination

a. Real Memory (First Example)
   1. "Close your eyes. Be present at a recent meal. Where are you? What are you eating? Is anyone else present? Be there now."
   2. "What do you see?"
   3. "What is the most distinct taste?"
   4. "What is the most distinct smell?"
   5. "What is the most distinct sound?"
   6. "What is the most distinct tecture or object you touched?"
   7. "What is your emotion?"
   8. "Where do you feel that emotion physically in your body?"
   9. "Do you know mentally even if you don't see or feel anything?"

b. Imagination (First Example)
   1. "Mickey Mouse eating your meal is one memory imposed on another

unless Mickey Mouse really was
eating that meal."

2. Ask questions two through nine listed under "a".

c. <u>Itemize the Differences between Memory and Imagination</u>

1. What were the most powerful characteristics of real memory? Was it the visual picture? The emotion? A knowing it is real?
2. Was that characteristic present or absent in the Mickey Mouse scene?
3. What are the differences between "a" and "b"?
4. Write down the characteristics of memory that made it real. Refer to this list and add to it when you do other exercises in this chapter.

<u>NOTES: MEMORY VS IMAGINATION</u>

Practice Exercise #2: Real Memory

a. "Select something memorable that hap-
    pened a few years ago. Be there now."
b. Ask questions 2 through 9 of Practice
    Exercise #1.
c. Again identify the characteristics of
    that memory and write them down.
d. Notice if they are the same or dif-
    ferent from those you listed in
    Practice Exercise #1.

Practice Exercise #3: Real Memory

a. "Close your eyes and remember coming
    into this room today. Retrace your
    steps. Recall everything you saw,
    felt, did etc. as you walked in.

b. Repeat questions 2 through 9 of Prac-
    tice Exercise #1. Do you experience
    the same characteristics of memory as
    in the previous practice exercises?
    Do they match or differ?

MORE NOTES: MEMORY VS IMAGINATION

EXERCISE II: FINDING YOUR BODY IN MEMORY

This exercise helps you locate yourself inside your body in a past life by experiencing in childhood in this lifetime how you locate yourself in your body. Stay inside your body looking out, NOT OUTSIDE LOOKING IN FROM THE MENTAL OBSERVER.

This exercise prepares you for getting into your own past life body in a past life regression. You experience what that feels like by going back to an early childhood memory in this lifetime. This helps demonstrate how you would know if you have been a famous personage, such as Napoleon, in a past life or had just seen him over there on his horse.

If you cannot see your own face or your face is stationery like a photo, and if you do not feel your own emotions inside your body, you are not in that body.

If you look out of your eyes at someone else and see their face moving naturally, while you are feeling your emotions inside your body, you are inside that body.

One major exception in past life regression is the moment of death, serious illness or traumatic accident, such as injury in war. It is possible to be out of body looking at yourself at such times to avoid pain in your physical body. "Near-death experiences" are like that. You see yourself from the mental observer. However, if it is your body, you can get back into it as easily as putting on your overcoat.

Practice Exercise: Finding Your Body in a Childhood Memory

a. "Close your eyes. Recall a group event in childhood in this lifetime such as a birthday or Christmas party. Choose an event that included strangers. Be in your body as a child. See the event through your eyes. Feel your emotions."

b. "Pretend you are inside the body of another child at the same event. Do not select your brother, sister or best friend. Select someone you were not emotionally close to. Can you see what he/she sees out of his/her eyes? Can you feel emotions inside his/her body? Do you see your own face? If so is it moving or still like a photo?

c. Write down your words e.g."I think the other child had a good time. I'm sad. My head hurts." Your words are clues to verify what you experienced. Words like "I think" mean "I don't know. I'm not the one experiencing it." Most people experience what they see with their eyes and feel with their emotions. They cannot experience someone else's emotions another's body.

d. A few people are very psychic and can experience entering and leaving another person's body. Entering and leaving are like walking in and out of a room. If you can do this, notice how you know you are not in another's body. Do you observe yourself and the other person from outside both bodies?

NOTES: FINDING MY BODY IN A MEMORY

EXERCISE III: DIFFERENCES BETWEEN INTUITION AND LOGIC

This exercise prepares you to develop intuition, which is a faster way of getting at the facts in a memory than step-by-step mental reasoning. Intuition is a right-brained, creative exercise which also helps locate past life memories speedily and effortlessly. Opening up the intuitive channel also enhances the individual's psychic and creative abilities to interpret the meaning of these experiences.

Intuition	Logic
a. Gut-level feeling, deep sense of knowing without prior thought or reasoning.	Analytical, intellectual, linear thought in logical sequence.
b. You "just know". It is a complete knowledge, but you don't know how you know.	Fact is proven by analysis of tangible evidence.
c. You have a strong emotional response or feeling.	You are unemotional or have muted emotions.
d. It comes in a flash, all at once, with no time to think first.	You figure out step-by-step using language.
e. Physical reactions (e.g. tense muscles).	No physical sensations.

The way to begin trusting your intuition is to accept the _first_ feeling, picture or words that pop into your head even if they don't make sense logically. Intuition is the channel of communication of the Higher Self. It is the "fast lane of the freeway". It gets you where you are going faster and with less effort. However, it takes practice to get used to it. It does not plod along. It gets answers spontaneously. So, it may make you feel you are not controlling the process, and that can feel scary. You have tuned in on the "wave length" of your Higher Self and your spirit guides. Learn to "get out of your own way" and let them do the work for you. That is what trusting the intuition is really all about.

Practice Exercise #1: Intuition

a. First Impressions (First Example)

   1. Give me your very first impression. The phone is ringing. You know who is calling before you pick up the receiver.

   2. Notice the sequence of events. Had you been thinking of that person? Did you have an emotional reaction when the phone rang? What thoughts ran through your mind?

b. Meeting Somebody (Second Example)

Go to a time when you met someone, perhaps for the first time, perhaps just for lunch. Be there now. Where are you meeting? Who got there first? What is the other person wearing? Do not try to remember. Accept what pops in even if it doesn't make sense.

c. Inspiration (Third Example)

Go to a time you had a great idea. Be there now. Where are you? What are you wearing? Do not try to remember. Accept what pops into your mind even if it doesn't make sense.

d. Identify Your Intuition

1. Picture
2. Emotional feeling
3. Physical reaction in your body
4. Thought in words running through your mind
5. Knowing without words (nonverbal)
6. Write down how you perceived your intuition in these three exercises.

Practice Exercise #2: Logic

a. Daily Routine (First Example)

Go to a time in your daily routine when you use logical reasoning e.g. looking up phone numbers or reading instructions. How do you know you are using logical reasoning?

b. Finding Your Way Here Today

Did you read a map or street signs? How do you use logical reasoning?

Practice Exercise #3: The Difference Between Intuition and Logic

a. Identify the characteristics of intuition.
b. Identify the characteristics of logic.
c. How do you know the difference between them?
d. Make a list on paper of those differences. Note that you perceived intuition the same way you perceived memory because memory comes to you intuitively.

NOTES: DIFFERENCES BETWEEN INTUITION AND LOGIC

EXERCISE IV - THOUGHT FORMS

You create images or impressions in your mind out of your emotions and beliefs. The ability to generate images simplifies and strengthens your perceptions about physical reality. Whether you are a visual person or not, you automatically generate thought forms. Please remember you do not have to see these images. You can know or sense or feel them.

In Metaphysics "thoughts are things". They have a physical reality much the way objects in your environment were ideas in your mind before you created them physically. This exercise has practical application to the past life regression. It zeroes in on a negative in this lifetime, which we are working to transmute, and locates a positive in the past life, which we are working to enhance and integrate in this life.

Thought forms also help you do the exercises in Chapter Three of this book. If you feel stuck or blocked, close your eyes and do a Thought Form. Do what you want with that Thought Form as long as you want to. Then, return to whatever written or meditative exercise you were doing. You will find it easier to do.

Practice Exercise - Thought Forms

Close your eyes. Go to a time when you felt an emotional feeling about something. Accept the first thought or feel- that pops into your mind. Concentrate.

Note the first <u>color</u> you see or know in
your mind. What is the shape of that
color? Size? Texture? Odor? Sound? Smell?
Is it rough or smooth? Hot or cold?
Moving or standing still? What emotion do
you feel about the Thought Form? Where in
your body do you feel this emotion? Ask
this question: What do I want to do with
the Thought Form? Accept the first answer
that pops into your mind.

Open your eyes. Write down a description
of the Thought Form and what you wanted
to do with it. Anytime you want you can
close your eyes and do that with your
Thought Form, over and over in your mind.
However, I caution you to stick to what
you got. Don't vary what you do with it.

EXAMPLES:

Yellow butterfly - I want to fly around
the house on its wings.

Purple and green tree - I want to kick
the purple trunk and hold green leaves.

<u>NOTES: THOUGHT FORMS</u>

MORE NOTES: THOUGHT FORMS

EXERCISE V - KARMA DRILL

Bad karma is any unresolved or unlearned lesson that results in negativity or blocks. Good karma is any resolved lesson because it fosters love, cooperation and inner security.

It is important to understand the purpose and significance of the Karma Drill. If you are critical of yourself or others, negativity comes back to you as negative effects. However, put out positive energy and you get positive energy back. What ye sow, so shall ye reap. With the Karma Drill, you are consciously changing negatives to positives.

When you begin this exercise, it may feel hypocritical to you if you are angry or have not been taught how to see positives in negative situations or people.

Practice Exercise - Karma Drill

a. Write down a negative thought you want to change.
b. Make a list of the benefits, advantages or lessons for you of having the negative. Choose simple things.
c. When you run out, stretch your list by adding one more benefit.

Practice the Karma Drill on simple things in your daily life. EXAMPLE: The person in front of you takes the last parking space in the lot. Ask yourself: "What are the benefits or advantages to me of that?" Start with a small benefit (e.g. "I can

park the car across the street.") Add
another (e.g. "I needed the exercise.")
Keep going. "I am early and can take
my time getting there." When you run
out, always add one more. "It is a
lovely day for a walk."

Next use a slightly more difficult
example, such as forgetting to do
something and having to make a special trip. Find the benefits or advantages of the negative. Always stretch
your list by adding one more after you
think you have run out.

Use the Karma Drill on increasingly
difficult situations. You will find it
works. The goal is to <u>identify whatever
positive attitudes feel real to you</u>
without denying your anger or any other
emotion. With practice, positive speech
and thought will more naturally become
a part of your daily life.

NOTES: KARMA DRILL

MORE NOTES: KARMA DRILL

SUMMARY

The Karma Drill trains your conscious mind to identify and validate positives in your daily experience. At the same time, the more you use the Karma Drill, the more you experience your intuition working for you. Work only with positives you can own or accept! Do not deny your anger or anxiety! Write notes about how you are feeling.

Trusting your intuition is often a difficult challenge. Students sometimes find themselves saying: "This doesn't make sense. That's not the way it happened." What helps to overcome your doubts is the following:

a. Practice the exercises distinguishing Intuition from Logic.

b. Enhance positive thought by using the Karma Drill frequently.

c. Enhance positive emotions by doing Thought Forms.

d. Never deny your feelings. Take the time to write down any thoughts and feelings you experience as you do exercises throughout this book.

In Chapter Two, you will learn other ways to break through your blocks.

CHAPTER TWO

WRITTEN PROBLEM-SOLVING

PROCESSES

CAUSE AND EFFECT PROCESS

You have begun accumulating notes about memories, thoughts and feelings that surfaced during the exercises in Chapter One. Thought Forms work at the emotional and intuitive levels. Karma Drill is both a mental and intuitive process. Each helped you begin to recognize some block or conflict or some unresolved problem in the present. Take the time to reread your notes and add to them whenever you like.

The next exercise builds on what you have done so far. It combines Thought Forms and the Karma Drill. You will need paper, pens and a quiet place to sit undisturbed.

In the first step, write down a belief or describe situation you want to change. Write a paragraph or more describing what is wrong and needs improvement.

In step two, you will do a Thought Form. Step two will help you remove or lessen a block that holds you back from finding a solution to the problem.

The following is how to do step two. Close your eyes. Think about the problem you want to solve. Let your thoughts and feelings surface. Don't fight them. (Do Thought Form Practice Exercise.) Once you answer the question, "What do I want to do with this Thought Form?", do that with your Thought Form over and over as long as you want to. Open your eyes.

Step three is next. Write down the solution to the problem. Do the best you can. Don't expect the problem to vanish spontaneously. If the exercise has given you an insight or has relieved some anxiety or decreased a negative feeling, it has done its job. Expect something to be unresolved. That is the material for the next step in this process.

In step four, close your eyes. Do a second Thought Form. This time, do the Thought Form on the positive new belief or resolution of the problem. Do what you want in your mind with your Thought Form as long as you want to. Open your eyes when you are ready. (This second Thought Form makes good homework.)

CAUSE AND EFFECT PROCESS
PRACTICE EXERCISE

1. Write down one belief or situation you want to change. Start with something simple. Each time examine something a little more difficult.

   EXAMPLE: I came to work this morning and found somebody else's car in my parking space. I had to park a block away. It made me late for work.

2. Do a Thought Form on what you wrote in step one. Close your eyes. Notice how you feel or what thoughts are in your head. Focus on the first color popping into your mind. Size? Shape? Taste? Smell? Sound? Texture?

Emotion about the Thought Form? What do you want to do with it? Do that with your Thought Form in your mind for a couple of minutes.

EXAMPLE: Red box. I want to kick it.

3. Write down what you would rather believe or what the solution to this problem is. Write a sentence or two.

4. Close your eyes. Do another Thought Form on the positive belief or the solution from step three. Do what you want with this Thought Form for several minutes.

EXAMPLE: Yellow Balloon. I fly around the world with it.

5. Do the second Thought Form as homework. Stick to the exact visual image and what you do with it. Do not free-associate with it. You are reinforcing positive resolution by repeating it.

CAUSE AND EFFECT PROCESS
WORKBOOK PAGES

1. Step One: Write a belief you want to change or describe a problem you want to solve.

2. Step Two: Do Thought Form Practice Exercise from Chapter One. Write the description of your Thought Form and what you did with it. Close your eyes. Do that with your Thought Form in your mind.

3. Step Three: State the belief you would rather have or the solution to the problem in Step One.

Step Four: Do another Thought Form. Write
down what it looks like and
what you did with it. Close
your eyes. Do that over and
over for several minutes.

Step Five: Do the second Thought Form as
homework. Do not change any of
the details. Do it as often as
you want to.

Step Six: Write down any thoughts or
feelings you are having now.
(More space on following
pages.)

NOTES: CAUSE AND EFFECT PROCESS

MORE NOTES: CAUSE AND EFFECT PROCESS

KARMA AND POSITIVE THOUGHT

"Energy follows thought" is a basic
metaphysical law. It means you create
your reality out of your beliefs; your
perspective colors the way you see and
therefore interact with the world. For
example, there are clouds in the sky.
Is the weather partly cloudy or partly
clear? Your answer, unless you are a
meteorologist, depends upon your perspective. If you believe it is partly
cloudy, you may be unwilling to risk a
picnic or a day at the beach in event
of rain. If you believe it is partly
clear, your expectation is the day will
probably turn out sunny. Belief and
expectation influence the way we think
and what we do.

Newton's Law (for every action, there
is an equal and opposite reaction) helps
us understand how belief and expectation
also affect our experience of the Law of
Karma, also known as the Law of Cause
and Effect. We react not only to events
occurring in this lifetime, but also past
life traumas. For example, people who put
down a particular ethnic, racial or religious group may become the victim of prejudice in a future life or may have a
revenge motive for prejudice experienced
in a past life. I have found in my past
life regression work individuals bigoted
in past lives often return in this life
as members of the group against which
they were prejudiced in a another life-.
time.

To say it another way: "As ye sow, so shall ye reap" and "Do unto others as you would have them do unto you". These are also statements of the Law of Karma. We create our reality out of our beliefs about life experience, and we can change our reality by changing the way we see the world. If our experience of reality has been negative, we can learn to change our perspective, which helps us create a positive, new experience resulting from our thought.

I add one word of caution. Where there are unresolved and unexpressed emotional feelings, particuarly anger, fear and guilt, changing one's beliefs will meet with resistance. That resistance is an indicator that deeper emotional work needs to be done before a positive experience of reality can be developed and healthy, productive ways of living can result. It is my experience that unresolved emotional issues frequently have past life roots, but I firmly believe it is important to begin by improving life in the here and now.

BLAME PROCESS

While doing Cause and Effect Process, you may have noticed a tendency to blame and be angry at certain people. Make notes on who they are and what they do or say that you criticize or blame. Notice what is the <u>focal point of your anger</u>. This will help you own what is causing your anger. Make notes about your feelings about this person or situation while you are doing the Blame Process.

The key to the Blame Process is taking responsibility for two things:

a. The negatives you project onto another person.
b. The positives that you identify are both in yourself and the person you blame or criticize.

The most important concept is SELF-RESPONSIBILITY, also called OWNERSHIP.

If you find yourself resistant to what you write down in Steps Two or Three, the Blame Process will be of great assistance to you. Notice your voice tone, facial expression, body language, and choice of words. They are clues to whether or not you are accepting responsibility for your anger towards another person or not.

Step one: Identify the person and the situation you blame or criticize. Make a written list of the negative character-istics of the person in that situation.

The first time you do this exercise, start with something simple, perhaps the grocery clerk who dropped your bag of groceries or the mechanic who said your car would be ready at 3:00 PM when it wasn't. As you get used to doing this process, select situations and people who are more important to you, such as family members or work associates.

Step Two: Go down each item of the list you wrote in Step One. Examine each item, one item at a time. Ask the following question of each item: "Have I ever done or said it, even once, to somebody else?" Even if the answer is, "Well, yes, once, twenty years ago," the answer is "yes". Put a check mark next to that item on your list and go on to the next item.

This represents ownership. It is like your signature at the bottom of the ownership certificate on your car. It says "this is mine". Ownership permits you to see how many of the things for which you blame or criticize others you have done or said yourself. Owning your anger is an important step toward resolving the problem you are working on.

At the same time, ownership can cause discomfort or even tears. You are learning to own your anger instead of projecting it onto someone else and then feeling victimized by what that person has done or said to you. This ownership does not diminish the wrongness you feel about their actions or words, and it does not make you wrong. It simply allows you to see that blame is a projection of your anger. What another person has said or done is not what makes you angry. It triggers off feelings you already have. Therefore, it brings that anger to the surface where you feel it and learn to deal with it instead of repressing it.

Step Three: Write a second list. It is a list of positive characteristics in the person you blame or criticize in Step One. Start with simple things. Don't discount anything. EXAMPLE: He wears nice clothes and is well groomed. EXAMPLE: He always remembers to wash his coffee cup when he is done.

Step Four: Go down each item in the second list. Examine each item, one item at a time. Ask the question: "Have I ever done or said that, even once, to somebody else?" Write "yes" or "no" next to each item on ths list.

If Steps Two or Three were difficult for you to do, Blame Process is helpful to you in owning your anger and converting blame to self-responsibility. I urge you to do Blame Process, over and over.

If Step Four is difficult for you, you blame yourself more than others. You have turned your anger inward against yourself. That is guilt. You may feel depressed or have low self-esteem. If so, I suggest Guilt and Lay Every Thought Upon the Heart Processes. They will benefit you more than Blame Process.

BLAME PROCESS
PRACTICE EXERCISE

1. Identify a person you blame or criticize. Describe a situation for which you blame or criticize this person. Make a list of the negative characteristics about this person in this situation.

   EXAMPLES: "He is always late."
   "He doesn't keep promises."
   "He is too demanding."

2. Take one item at a time from your list. Ask this question: "Have I ever said or done this, even once, to somebody other than the person I am blaming?" Go down every item on your list, one item at a time. Answer "yes" or "no".

   EXAMPLES: "Yes, I was late yesterday."
   "Yes, I forgot to do something I promised last week."
   "No, I have never been a demanding person."

3. Make a second list. Indicate the positive characteristics about the person you have been blaming or criticizing.

   EXAMPLE: "He always says good morning."

4. Go down the second list, one item at a time. Ask the question: "Have I done or said it even once to someone else?

   EXAMPLE: "I always say good morning."

BLAME PROCESS
WORKBOOK PAGES

1. Write a list of characteristics you dislike or criticize in the person you blame or are critical of:

2. Go back over every item in the list in Step One, one item at a time, and put "yes" next to each item you own about yourself. To find out which you own, ask yourself this question: "Have I ever done or said this, even once, to somebody else, other than the person I criticize?" If the answer is "yes" to "even once," the answer is "yes".

3. Make a second list. Indicate the characteristics you like or consider positive in the person you criticize.

4. Go down the second list, one item at a time. Ask yourself: "Have I ever done or said that, even once to somebody else other than the person I am criticizing?" If the answer is "yes," write "yes" in front of the item in Step Three. Do this to every item.

5. Take time to write down your feelings and thoughts about this person or the situation or anything else you may be thinking of right now.

A NOTE ABOUT ANGER

Anger is not inherently bad. It is a
legitimate emotion. Nothing is wrong
with being angry. It is only "wrong" to
have no constructive way to express it.

If someone steals my purse, I feel angry.
I demand to get it back. If I could not
get it back, I may need to complain to
someone who could get it back for me
(e.g.) a policeman. If unavailable, I may
want to beat up on my pillow. If I steal
someone else's purse, it is an inappropriate demonstration of my anger. Why
should someone else be victimized? It

would be better if I had an appropriate place to act out my anger.

An example of an appropriate place for my anger might be a Thought Form on how angry I am. I might get a Thought Form I want to blast to pieces or kick into the ocean. That is a healthy release.

Anger often creates destructive patterns of behavior if not expressed in productive ways. Examples are revenge, envy, jealousy and pure rage. A person having a difficult time handling anger is well advised to seek the aid of a therapist.

NOTES ABOUT NOTE TAKING

When you have done the Blame Process several times, you will probably notice one person or situation keeps surfacing. This pattern will reappear in different forms throughout this course. Take time to make notes about your thoughts and feelings. Keep your notes together in a notebook. Write the date of each entry. This is a good way to start a journal.

You may not know why you feel upset. It is useful to go back to Chapter One and do Thought Forms on your block. Acting out against Thought Forms helps ventilate feelings. Do this when you feel angry, anxious or blocked. Then, use Cause and Effect Process to clarify what is bothering you. Then, do Blame Process, again. This sequence will help you better understand what has made you feel upset.

GUILT PROCESS

In doing Blame Process, you may get stuck doing Step Four. If so, go back to positive items (second list). Notice which ones you could not own about yourself. Take one item at a time and do Guilt Process on it. You might be surprised what memories it generates for you to work on.

Guilt is often generated when you attempt an inappropriate solution to a real problem. When you find a more appropriate solution, guilt often drops away.

> EXAMPLE: Imagine teenage boys are friends. The older boys urge the younger one to do something daring to prove he's a man. Perhaps, the dare is to steal something from a store. The younger boy feels conflicted. He has been taught not to steal, but he wants the approval of the older boys. So, he steals CD's. Unable to reconcile the act with his beliefs, he fantasizes the store owner did not see him do it. In reality, the store owner didn't see him or he would have made him return the CD's or called the police. If he is not caught, he carries a load of guilt.

The boy's guilt derives from an inappropriate solution to a real problem. He wanted the other boys to accept him as a grown-up. Peer pressure is a very real issue. However, stealing is not an appropriate solution. The boy needed a more appropriate way of getting recognition.

Guilt is not always felt as an emotional conflict. It can be experienced as a conflict between two mental beliefs.

EXAMPLE: Let's say you believe in reincarnation because you have had a past life memory. However, let's say you were brought up with religious training that disavows reincarnation. Perhaps, you were made to feel guilty if you believed what you believed. This could have caused a conflict. Perhaps, you recently read a book on past lives and found yourself torn between accepting your early religious training or your belief in reincarnation.

When you feel guilty about something or have a mental conflict between two different beliefs, remember that guilt often derives from an inappropriate solution to a real problem or need. Identify the real problem and find an appropriate solution. Guilt often drops away.

GUILT PROCESS
PRACTICE EXERCISE

1. Identify a SITUATION in this lifetime where you feel you hurt another person (physically, emotionally or mentally). Then, answer two questions:
   a) Who do you FEEL you hurt?
   b) How do you FEEL you hurt him/her?

2. What do you feel guilty about? If you do not feel guilty, describe a conflict you experienced between your beliefs and your actions.

EXAMPLE: You do not believe in cheating
but you did not return change
the clerk overpaid you.

3. Who NEARLY OR ACTUALLY FOUND OUT what
you did? If you are unsure how to answer this question, write down the name
of the person you fear MIGHT KNOW,
ACTUALLY DOES KNOW, or YOU MOST WANT
TO PREVENT KNOWING THE TRUTH.

4. Describe THE REAL PROBLEM you were
actually trying to solve with this
inappropriate solution. (If you have
difficulty identifying what this problem actually is, do Step Five before
doing Step Four.)

5. Close your eyes. Do a Thought Form.
Act out your frustration, anxiety or
block against the Thought Form. Open
your eyes. Write down a description
of the Thought Form, what you wanted
to do with it, and any other thoughts
and feelings you are experiencing.

a) Do Step Four, again.

b) If you are still stuck, do Lay
Every Thought Upon the Heart Process on the situation you described
in Step One of Guilt Process. Both
help you in problem resolution.

GUILT PROCESS
WORKBOOK PAGES

1. Write a description of the situation where you <u>FEEL</u> you hurt someone, did something wrong or felt conflicted between your beliefs and actions.

a) NAME the person you FEEL you hurt.

b) Indicate HOW you feel you hurt that person.

2. What do you feel guilty about? If you do not feel guilty, describe the conflict you experienced between your belief and action in this situation.

3. Name the person who nearly or actually found out or you most want to prevent from knowing about this situation.

4. Identify the real problem you want
   to solve. CIRCLE THE KEY WORDS IN
   YOUR ANSWER TO STEP FOUR. They will
   give you important clues about how to
   test reality. Reality-testing is often
   the first step to overcoming the fears
   and dissolving fantasies often associated with guilt. (If you can't do Step
   Four, do Step Five instead.)

5. Do a Thought Form and act out your
   frustration or anxiety against your
   Thought Form. Write down a description of your Thought Form, what you
   did with it, and any feelings you had.
   Once you have done Step Five, go back
   and try Step Four, again.

6. If you still can't do Step Four, do
   Lay Every Thought Upon the Heart Process to examine the situation you described in Step One of Guilt Process.

ADDITIONAL NOTES: GUILT PROCESS

CIRCLE/LIST EXERCISE

Are you feeling angry, depressed or anxious right now? Has the work up to this point unleashed a lot of feelings, thoughts and perhaps some memories of people and events you may not have thought of for a long time? Did you get stuck in one of the previous exercises and find yourself unable to do one of them? If so, the Circle/List Process is tailor-made for you.

The goal of this exercise is to write down every word that pops into your mind in the sequence it pops in. Write every word even though some words don't seem related to the subject you are working on. Don't leave out words as irrelevant. This is "stream of consciousness" writing. Everything is relevant even when it seems irrelevant.

In Step One, write a word, phrase or somebody's name in the middle of a circle or at the top of a piece of paper.

EXAMPLE:

Remember: write down every word that pops into your mind. Either write them like spokes of a wheel around the circle or in a column beneath the word heading the list.

EXAMPLE:

ANGER

Anger	Anger
Mother	Love
It's hot in here.	Hate
What time is it?	Green
This is foolish?	Pink
Help!	No, No, No!
	Stop it!
	That hurts.

As you look at your list, pick the word, name or words that "pushes buttons" with you or to which you have a reaction. Put it at the top of a page or inside a circle. Write every word that pops into your mind. Repeat the exercise as often as you want until you feel calmer.

CIRCLE/LIST PROCESS
PRACTICE EXERCISE

1. Take a sheet of paper. Write a word, name or phrase that is upsetting you at the top of the page or in a circle. Write EVERY word or phrase at random even if it makes no sense.

2. Continue doing this exercise over and over until you feel calmer. Don't try to analyze the meaning. Just write! Do this exercise on a workbook page.

CIRCLE/LIST EXERCISE
WORKBOOK PAGE

A NOTE ABOUT NOTETAKING

Circle/List Process is safe ventilating.
You can do it anywhere, any time to let
off steam quickly. You can do it while
you are waiting for someone who is late.
Put the name in the middle of circle or
top of a list and do this exercise. All
you need is pen and paper. Remember to
write EVERY word that pops into your
head even it is doesn't make sense. Do
this exercise until you feel calmer. It
is a good way to express your anger.

Circle/List Process is also productive
to use while doing other exercises in
this WORKBOOK. Grab pen and paper when
you feel blocked, anxious, fearful or
angry. Let off steam before you go on
to the next step.

It is common for this exercise to bring
up thoughts and feelings because it uses
free association. Thoughts may suddenly
pour from your pen. Carry a notebook and
write them down. As always, they will
provide material for you to work on in
the next process in this WORKBOOK.

BROKEN RECORD PROCESS

One of the most common stumbling blocks to success in solving problems and creating what you want is unwillingness many people have to assert themselves. People who do not express their needs and feelings about a situation at the time it is happening often feel frustrated, isolated and cheated later on. By contrast, identifying your needs and wants and vocalizing them at appropriate times to appropriate people replaces isolation and powerlessness with feelings of satisfaction, belonging and mastery.

The key to self-expression is using "I" statements (e.g. "I feel" and "I want"). Saying the word "I" does NOT mean you are selfish, although many people have been conditioned to believe it does. In fact, the word "I" represents "self-responsibility" or "ownership". It indicates you are voicing your legitimate right to say how you feel and what you want. Learning to use the word "I" in self-expression is a crucial step towards self-assertion.

I recommend practicing this exercise in front of a mirror at home. Say your "I feel" and "I want" statements without dropping your gaze. Speak clearly and repeat your words 10 minutes or more a day before you talk to the person. Practice makes it easier to confront them. "I" statements make it clear you are not putting them on the defensive or making them "the bad guy". This exercise gets results. Try it!

If you find it scary to confront the person no matter how long you practiced in front of a mirror or if you find it scary to vocalize your feelings in front of a mirror even when you are alone, you are being paralyzed by fear. Your emotional issue is deeper than learning to communicate assertively. It may indicate psychotherapy would help you work through your fears about the relationship with the person you are afraid to confront.

BROKEN RECORD PROCESS
PRACTICE EXERCISE

1. STATEMENT OF FACT: First, make a factual statement about the situation.

2. STATEMENT OF FEELINGS: Then, assert your emotion. Use the words: "I feel".

3. STATEMENT OF WANTS OR DESIRES: Finally state what you want. Use these words: "I want" - "I would like" - "I prefer".

EXAMPLES:

Fact: It is hot in this room
Feeling: I feel (angry) (frustrated) that you always keep the room so hot.
Desire: I would like you to turn down the thermostat to 68°.

Fact: It is raining very hard, and my car's tires are worn thin.
Feeling: I feel afraid to drive my car in this weather.
Desire: I want to change my appointment to Tuesday.

BROKEN RECORD
WORKBOOK PAGES

1. Statement of Fact

2. Statement of "I feel"

3. Statement of "I want" or I prefer"

4. Write down notes about your thoughts
   and feelings practicing this process.
   (Blank notetaking page follows.)

ADDITIONAL NOTES: BROKEN RECORD

LAY EVERY THOUGHT UPON THE HEART PROCESS

This is the most important written process in this WORKBOOK. It is based upon the sound metaphysical theory that a solution to a problem where everybody wins is the best solution. It teaches love and cooperation. That is more productive than a win-lose philosophy and is also therapeutic.

An aggressive, angry person who needs to win at the expense of others often has difficulty with Step 2 (b) and is afraid of losing control and feeling powerless.

A person who is acting out a victim or martyr script will have difficulty doing Step 2 (a) and is afraid of being powerful and taking responsibility for his/her decisions. He/she may also fear making mistakes and not being perfect. "Martyrs" do not get to do what they really want to do. They tend to go along with what others want to avoid disapproval.

"Everybody wins" solutions are a practical alternative to either the aggressor or the martyr script. "Everybody wins" solutions require three things:

    a. Learning how to HEAR what another person needs.
    b. Learning how to ASSERT your own needs without putting someone else down for his/her beliefs.
    c. Learning how to NEGOTIATE A COMPROMISE among differing needs; EVERYONE GETS SOME of what he/she wants.

Solving problems with "everybody wins" solutions creates cooperation and replaces inner conflict with calmness and a sense of belonging. If you still feel angry or cheated after completing Lay Every Thought Upon the Heart Process, go back and do it again. If you do not feel calmer the second time, you are not getting something you need and want. Check the martyr and "everybody wins" solutions. They should be different. If they are the same, they are both martyr scripts. You have not yet found an "everybody wins" solution.

Step One: State the problem or conflict to be resolved. Write it down on a sheet of paper.

Step Two: FIND THREE DIFFERENT SOLUTIONS:
a. You get what you want at the expense of another person.
b. The other person gets what he/she wants at your expense.
c. Each person gets something even if it is not everything he/she wants.

If the third solution "feels right," it is an "everybody wins" solution. That is what is meant by "laying every thought upon the heart". It has to "feel right" when you are done or you have not found an "everybody wins" solution.

Remember: You are the one who is doing this process. The only thing that counts right now is how the "everybody wins" FEELS TO YOU. Please do not try to put yourself in someone else's shoes.

LAY EVERY THOUGHT UPON THE HEART PROCESS
PRACTICE EXERCISE

1. Identify the problem or conflict you want to resolve and name the participants in this situation.

2. Devise Three Alternative Solutions:
   a. A solution in which you win and everyone else loses or fails. (Aggressor or Controller Script.)
   b. A solution in which others win and you lose or fail. (Martyr or Victim Script.)
   c. A solution in which everybody wins or gains something even if it is not the whole amount he/she wants.
      EXAMPLE: You want to eat Chinese food for dinner. I want to eat Italian. We send out for both. Each of us eats the food he/she wants.

3. When you have concluded this process, answer this question: "What events might occur to prevent this agreement from succeeding?"

4. Take the time to write down your thoughts and feelings. Continue to do the Lay Every Thought Upon the Heart Process on any answers you get to Question Three. Removing these blocks will help you uncover an "everybody wins" solution.

LAY EVERY THOUGHT UPON THE HEART PROCESS
WORKBOOK PAGES

1. Write down a description of the problem or conflict you want to resolve.

2. Create three alternative solutions:

   a. Aggressor Script (I win, you lose):

   b. Martyr/Victim Script (You win, I lose):

c. Everybody Wins Solutions: List as many
   as you want. Then, ask: "How does this
   answer feel?" If it doesn't feel right,
   it isn't an "everyone wins" solution.

3. Now, write down the first words that
   pop into your mind AFTER you ask this
   question: "What events might occur to
   prevent this solution from succeeding?"
   List as many answers as you get.

4. Repeat Lay Every Thought Upon the
   Heart Process on each item in Step 3
   until each problem has been solved.

ADDITIONAL NOTES: LAY EVERY THOUGHT UPON THE HEART

KARMA AND PROBLEM SOLVING

There is good karma, and there is bad karma. In the simplest terms, good karma rewards, and bad karma feels like punishment. There is no area in which I have found it to be more true than in problem resolution. We live in a results-oriented country. What works, sells. Karmically, good karma is a resolved problem or a lesson that has been learned. Bad karma is an unresolved problem or lesson that has not been learned.

Changing one's relationship with someone by doing a cognitive, written exercise like this one identifies what is wrong and how it might be corrected. This is practical and spiritual. We may be more rapidly overcoming something that could otherwise have taken lifetimes of trial and error. Like high-speed technology, karmic lesson-learning is accelerated by cognitive processes. If you are ready to engage in accelerated learning, you "get your karma back faster".

A NOTE ABOUT NOTETAKING

Lay Every Thought Upon the Heart Process may generate a lot of negative reactions and a desire to write a lot of notes. If that is what you experience, you probablydiscovered a martyr script as the way you try to solve problems. You may feel angry you have accepted the belief you are supposed to be self-sacrificing, so others can get what they want at your expense. If this describes you, take time out to ventilate your thoughts and feelings on paper NOW! Pay special attention to what feels wrong about the solution(s) you get in this exercise.

Remember there are three components to finding "everybody wins" solutions. Go back and review those three components. If any one is missing, everyone did NOT win (and that particularly means YOU!) If you are the one who lost out, figure out why. Then, go back and find an "everybody wins" solution that feels right to you.

This is a good exercise to do in a group. The suggestions of other people can help give you a different perspective on how to get an "everybody wins" solution. When you have achieved it, you will feel the difference. It promotes mutual coopera- tion and a sense of inner harmony.

Meantime, I suggest you do further work in the following three areas:
a. ACTIVE LISTENING - This helps you hear what another person is actually saying.
b. ASSERTIVE COMMUNICATION - This helps you learn to vocalize to others what you really want from them.
c. NEGOTIATION SKILLS - This helps you learn to create compromises that achieve at least part of what you really want in a given situation.

Books and classes on all three are available at college extensions and in other adult education programs.

MANIFESTATION PROCESS

"Manifestation" is the process of creating something in physical reality. The
word was originally intended to mean
bringing an aspect of spiritual purpose
or Dharma into physical existence. The
Manifestation Process is very helpful
for providing "successes" or "concrete
results" in your daily life. It can be
applied to fixing your roof or deciding
where to go on vacation. It can also be
applied to bringing your spiritual goals
into physical manifestation. When you
gain mastery over routine things, manifestation of spiritual goals comes more
easily.

It is common to have big plans that never
manifest. This exercise can help you find
out why. Often, the truth is you don't
want to do what you say you want to do.
Your realization of that truth may be
blocked by a fear that is also blocking
manifestation. That fear may be layered
over with a lot of mental excuses or
objections (as they say in sales) about
why the "plan" cannot work. Your subconscious mind has not been asked to express
its opinion. If it had, it would not lie.
Manifestation Process will help you find
out what the truth is and how to create
in the physical universe what you really
want to create, not what you may think
you want to create.

Step One: Write down what you believe
          you want to do or create.

Step Two: State the PURPOSE of doing that. This step answers the question: "Why do I want to do that?"

Step Three: Identify your PLAN OF ACTION for achieving this goal. It should be stated is one short phrase or sentence with no real detail. It answers the questions: "What do I want to do?"

EXAMPLE:

Step One: Going to Europe for 3 weeks.

Step Two: PURPOSE of this trip is to experience cultures other than your own.

Step Three: PLAN is to spend one week each in London, Paris and Rome in off-season (maybe September). Travel alone.

The next two steps identify what stops your plan from manifesting.

Step Four: A list of mental excuses or reasons why you cannot do it.

Mental excuses can often be eliminated using Lay Every Thought Upon the Heart Process because they are problems that can be solved.

Step Five: A list of emotional blocks to getting what you say you want.

Emotional blocks can often be identified
by accepting the spontaneous answer to a
simple question: "What am I afraid of?"
The key is to accept and write down the
first words that pop into your head after
this question even if your next reaction
is to discount what you just thought. The
answer you get may surprise you or may
not make sense to you, but the unconscious will not lie to you. Accepting
the first thought that pops into your
mind helps you get past ego defenses
that otherwise block your looking at
the truth.

If emotionally you are still not ready
to manifest or even to begin what you
say you want to do, there are several
possible ways of approaching the problem.
You might try exercises like the Broken
Record Process, Circle/List Process,
Cause and Effect Process and Thought
Forms on feeling blocked or not wanting
to carry out the PLAN. These are examples of ventilating exercises, which
may make it easier for you to accept
the truth your unconscious is trying
to tell you.

Step Six: Identify the FORM by which
          you will carry out the PLAN.
          This step answers the ques-
          tion: "How do I do that?"

FORM includes all the details you left
out of Step Three (PLAN). For example,
FORM would include making plane and hotel
reservations, budgeting time and money,
getting a Eurorail pass, mapping out your

itinerary, stopping home delivery of your newspaper, arranging for mail to be kept at the post office until you returned.

It is important to understand how PLAN and FORM differ. Many people have a tough time distinguishing them.

a) PLAN is what to do. It can be summed up in one sentence.

b) FORM is how to do it. It involves the minute details for carrying out PLAN.

Usually, the blocks to manifestation are unconscious and emotional. You may unconsciously be hanging onto failure, avoiding mastery or experiencing fear preventing you from facing something about yourself and your beliefs, which are changing. I especially urge you to pay attention to the answers you got in Step Five ("What am I afraid of?").

Once you change your beliefs consciously, you should be able to manifest what you really want. If you have tried these exercises and are still blocked, reputabe counseling or psychotherapy may help you break through in ways you have been unable to accomplish on your own.

If you are looking for a professional trained in past life therapy, you can contact the Association for Past Life Research and Therapies (APRT), P.O. Box 20151, Riverside, CA 92516. Phone: (714) 784-1570. APRT can provide referrals in your area.

MANIFESTATION PROCESS
PRACTICE EXERCISE

1. State what you want to create or do or describe the problem you want to solve.

2. Detail the PURPOSE of doing it and answer the question: "Why do I want to do it?"

3. Describe your PLAN OF ACTION in one or two brief sentences.

   EXAMPLE: Two-week vacation backpacking in the Sierras followed by one week in San Francisco.

4. List every mental excuse for not doing this:

   EXAMPLES: I don't have enough money.
   I don't have enough time.
   I don't want to backpack by myself.

   Use Lay Every Thought Upon the Heart Process to solve each problem in your list and eliminate your excuses.

5. Find the strongest emotions associated with each block or excuse by writing down what pops into your mind after you ask: "What am I afraid of?"

   a. Take time to write down your thoughts and feelings before you go further with this process.

b. Typical fears that often arise here:

Fear of failure and fear of success
   (often associated with each other)
Fear of physical pain, being harmed,
   dying, losing something or someone
Fear of risk, adventure, the unknown
Fear in general (high anxiety level)
Fear of being a competent adult who
         can do things for him/herself.

6. Identify the FORM in which you want
   to carry out your PLAN.

   EXAMPLE: List phone numbers and times
            you can reach vendors, names
            and addresses of stores that
            carry materials you need,
            store hours, exact cost of
            supplies, an outline of how
            to manage your time and pay
            for the things you need.

7. Any answer you write down in Step Five
   will make good material for what you
   do in Chapter Three of this WORKBOOK,
   especially NEEDS OF THE CHILD. So,
   I suggest you write a note next to
   your answer in Step Five saying:
   "Reread this answer before doing
    NEEDS OF THE CHILD PROCESS."

MANIFESTATION
<u>WORKBOOK PAGES</u>

1. Write down what you want to do:

2. Identify the PURPOSE of doing this.
   Answer the question: "Why do I want
   to do it?"

3. Identify your PLAN OF ACTION in one
   or two short sentences:

4. Write down all the mental excuses why you cannot do this. Then, find a solution to each problem in your list. Use Lay Every Thought Upon the Heart Process if you have difficulty solving a problem:

Excuse/Problem   Solution

a.

b.

c.

d.

5. Answer this question : "What am I afraid of?". Write down the first words that pop into your mind even if you do not feel any fear.

   (REREAD YOUR ANSWER TO THIS QUESTION BEFORE YOU DO NEEDS OF THE CHILD PROCESS IN CHAPTER THREE.)

Write down any additional thoughts or feelings you are having right now.

6. Write down all the minute details of
   FORM needed to manifest your PLAN:

ADDITIONAL NOTES: MANIFESTATION PROCESS

KARMA AND MANIFESTATION

The laws of manifestation are primarily intended for carrying out at the physical plane one's Dharma or Spiritual Purpose or what we are here to give back to the Universe. Like any lofty goal, one needs practice to reach it. Human beings need to practice their miracles a long time before they get the hang of how to make them look spontaneous and easy.

So, Manifestation Process is intended to be such practice. It is intended to be used on such mundane things as fixing the roof, painting the garage, buying a new car, and planning a vacation. It can best be started by removing the little stumbling blocks of life, such as cleaning out the hall closet and asking for help to do it. I believe Manifestation Process must start simply before it is possible to entertain thoughts of inventing the world's best mousetrap.

Manifestation helps you master your karmic lessons. It helps identify what you believe you want to do. It also identifies what blocks to success exist and how to find out whether you really want to do instead of what you think you want to do.

Karmically, Manifestation Process is a good way to find out if you are on course or need a course correction in the matter of mastering your karmic lessons and being on your Spiritual Purpose.

CHAPTER THREE

MEDITATIVE
and
SPOKEN
PROCESSES

DRAMA PROCESS

This exercise is intended to help you act out a scene as if you were on a stage. It is "ad lib" theater. Speaking out loud and acting out the roles in a "drama" in your life are good ways of getting a handle on an emotional crisis. The idea is to pretend you are in a play and you are playing all the roles in this play. Don't be shy! There are no theatrical agents in the audience. This is fun!

Start with a story that is actually going on in your life now. Pick a situation that involves only 2 or 3 characters. Stand up. Push back the chairs. Give yourself room to move around as you act. Maybe you had an argument at breakfast or your secretary raised a fuss at the office or your Little League Manager refused to let you coach next year. Whatever it is, pick a situation.

Now, stand up. Go "on stage". Move around. Be each person in the skit. If the character is sitting over there, move over there and sit where he/she is supposed to sit. If the next character is standing in the doorway, get up and move to the doorway. Move around. Act out all the roles. Be all the characters.

You can make up lines. You don't have to remember exactly what each one actually said. Say: "Nellie, come over here." Don't say: "Bill said, 'Nellie, come over here'." You are playing each person. Speak everyone's lines. This is "ad lib" theater!

When the skit is over, sit down. Take out
pen and paper. Your next task is to analyze the lessons learned by doing this
skit. First, write down what each person
learned. Next, write down how each person
helped the others learning their lessons
even if that person was resisting you.
Being able to see this is the real reason
this process is most successful acted out
loud in front of a group. They see things
you may not see.

The goal of the exercise is rescripting.
That means changing the ending. Once you
know the lessons, you can identify alternative behavior. The new ending is then
acted out in place of the previous dysfunctional one. That's right! You get
back on stage! (If you find you are
really stuck doing this exercise, do
Lay Every Thought Upon the Heart and
Manifestation Processes in the previous
chapter. Both exercises help you identify
new ways to solve the problem and carry
out the new solution.)

EXAMPLE: ARGUMENT AT BREAKFAST
Johnny wants the car. Dad promised it to
him but changed his mind. Johnny learns
responsibility. Dad learns to communicate
his intentions clearly. Dad's resistance
to Johnny's having the car helps teach
Johnny people have the right to change
their minds. Johnny's upset helps Dad
express his feelings. The moral of the
story for both of them is to communicate
their needs instead of letting things
slide into a crisis.

DRAMA PROCESS
PRACTICE EXERCISE

1. ## The Drama

   a. ### Description

      1) What title would you give this play?
      2) What is the plot or story?
      3) Who are the main characters?

   b. ### Acting

      1) What does each character do? Act out each role.
      2) Speak in the first person and move around the stage.
      3) Address the other characters in the first person.
      4) Don't say "he/she said".
      5) THIS IS THEATER!

2. ## Mental Analysis

   a. Sit down and write.
   b. What is the moral or lesson of this play?
   c. What lesson is each one supposed to be learning? Identify 1 lesson per character. YOU ARE SEEING EACH PERSON'S LESSONS THROUGH YOUR EYES.
   d. How does each person help each of the others learn his/her lessons even if someone resists learning?

3. <u>Rewriting the Script</u>

   a. Rewrite the play with a positive
      ending. How would it be different
      if everyone learned their lessons?

      (Use Lay Every Thought Upon the
      Heart Process here if you need
      help with rescripting.)

   b. Stand up and act out the play
      again, but use the new ending.
      Speak each part in the script
      the first person. You are all
      the actors.

   c. Sit down and write out a plan to
      carry out this new script in your
      relationship with these people.

      (Use the Manifestation Process.)

4. If it feels too scary to act out this
   process in front of others right now,
   write the steps on paper, first. When
   you are ready, then act it out loud.
   It is more powerful to speak roles
   out loud in the first person and be
   all the characters. FEELING AND
   EXPERIENCE ARE THE BEST TEACHERS!

DRAMA PROCESS
WORKBOOK PAGES

1. Write down the title of your play.

2. In a sentence, describe the story or "plot" of your play.

3. Name the characters. List no more than three including yourself.

   a.

   b.

   c.

4. Now act it out. Get on stage. Move the furniture. Play all the roles. This is theater!

5. Mental Analysis:

   a. What is the moral of the story? In a sentence or two summarize "the nugget" of what this is all about?

"Moral of the Story" (cont.)

b. What lesson is each character
   supposed to be learning? Remember
   you are looking at this through
   your own eyes and experience.

   <u>CHARACTER</u>   <u>LESSON</u>

   1)

   2)

   3)

c. How does each character in this play help every other character learn his/her lessons even if he/she resists learning?

    1) Character No. 1:

        a) How he/she helps character number 2:

        b) How he/she helps character number 3:

    2) Character No. 2:

        a) How he/she helps character number 1:

        b) How he/she helps character number 3:

3) Character No. 3:

   a) How he/she helps character
      number 1:

   b) How he/she helps character
      number 2:

6. Rewrite the script of this play with
   a positive ending. How would things
   work out differently if the actors
   learned their lessons?

7. Remember, if it feels too scary to
   act out loud, you can write the
   answers on paper.

Additional Notes: Drama Process

A NOTE ABOUT NOTETAKING

Sometimes, the Drama Process feels scary to do before your have tried it. Some people experience anticipatory anxiety about expressing themselves. If you are feeling this way, give yourself permission to write instead of act. However, if you decide to try acting, you will probably find thoughts and feelings surfacing. Write them down after doing this exercise. This is "ventilating" and it will make you feel better.

You may also experience resistance to carrying out the new script that came up in the Drama Process. You may make mental excuses why your solution won't work. If so, go back and repeat Circle/ List Exercise, Thought Forms, Needs of the Child, Lay Every Thought Upon the Heart and Manifestation Processes.

Writing your thoughts and feelings after each exercise is like keeping a journal. It expresses your feelings and helps you resolve problems. Buy a big 8"x11" notebook and write in it frequently as you work throughout this book.

INSIGHT INTO PAST LIFE REGRESSION

Drama Process and Past Life Regression are like a movie or stage play going on inside your mind. You are the main character, and the story is about you. Drama Process explores an incident in this lifetime the way regression explores past lives. Both help you learn lessons.

Karmically, this makes sense. The only person you can change is you. You cannot live another person's life. You cannot take on the other person's Karma. Drama Process like Past Life Regression helps you experience you are you. Your perspective is the only one you can change. If another chooses to change in response to changes you are making, that is their choice. However, you have not changed them, no matter how much you care about them or want to help them. You can only work on changing you. Both Drama and Past Life Regression help you experience that.

NEEDS OF THE CHILD PROCESS

People who experienced emotional hurt and pain in childhood are often emotionally blocked as adult. They want to change the "script" about childhood traumas. Needs of the Child Process is effective for identifying "dramas" and breaking through emotional blocks. One helpful way to use this exercise is to substitute Needs of the Child Process for Section Two (Mental Analysis) of Drama Process.

Here's how to make this exercise work for you. Close your eyes. Relax. Describe the _first_ memory from childhood that pops spontaneously into your mind when you do Needs of the Child. Do not edit! _First memory_! _Allow yourself to be that child_!

Once you are experiencing that memory, ask yourself the following two questions:

1. What did you want as the child in that situation?

2. From whom did you want this?

Trust your first, spontaneous responses. Let yourself cry. Rewrite the script. This time the child asks for and gets what he/she wants.

Do the best you can. You may find it difficult to experience receiving what you really wanted and perhaps did not get as a child.

You may also be surprised at what you really wanted. It is often different from what you, the adult, thought you wanted as a child.

Allow your first impressions to be the source of your experience in doing this exercise.

Also, notice whether it is difficult or easy for you to get what you want from whom you want it in doing this exercise.

The key to making Needs of the Child Process work for you is to understand the meaning of your first impressions:

1. As a child in this exercise, if you get spontaneously what you want from whom you want it, you have resolved something in your relationship with that person.

2. If you cannot, as the child, get what you want from whom you want it in this exercise, something is unresolved in this relationship. Trust your first impressions.

KARMA AND THE CHILD

If you experienced emotional hurt or were victimized in childhood in this lifetime, you probably have had past lives in which you played out the same script. You also may have had one or more "Karmic Cause" past lives in which you did to others what you experienced in this lifetime. That does not make you a bad person nor are you being punished. A karmic pattern exists to help you learn the lesson and resolve a painful problem.

Karmic Astrology gives further credence to this idea. Relationships with mother and father figures in this lifetime are reflected by two "planets": Moon and Saturn. Moon represents mother and women of importance. Saturn reflects authority figures (male or female). Moon and Saturn are always karmic and reveal in the birth chart unresolved past life lessons brought into this life from past lives.

Needs of the Child Process locates key incidents from childhood and provides an experience of a childhood memory even if you do not consciously remember it. It also gives you a sense of how past life memories become conscious in past life regression. Needs of the Child helps you experience how past life recall feels.

FINDING YOUR KARMIC BLOCK, THE MAJOR LESSON YOU ARE HERE TO LEARN

Before you begin doing Needs of the Child Process, find your answers to the following questions and write them down here:

1) LAY EVERY THOUGHT UPON THE HEART PROCESS - item 3 (page 79):

2) MANIFESTATION PROCESS - item 5 (page 93) "What am I afraid of?":

3) DRAMA PROCESS - item 6 (page 106) - rewriting the script with a positive ending. If it was difficult to accept the new ending, write down what was difficult for you to accept:

Now, reread all three answers you have written on this page.

As you do Needs of the Child Process, notice whether you can get what you want from whom you want it as the child in this exercise. If you cannot, the ego state of the child within you fears being denied, rejected, punished or abandoned by an angry parent figure. You may have suppressed anger at the parent for denying or hurting you. Until this anger is resolved, you will not be able to manifest what you want as an adult. However, it is no longer your parent's "fault". You have internalized their message or script and made it your own. Needs of the Child Process helps you zero in on situations where that script was acted out and your emotional pain began.

REMOVING YOUR KARMIC BLOCK

To change your karmic script, you have to know what block you internalized and how to own it as yours. It manifests in 3 places in exercises in this chapter:

(1) NEEDS OF THE CHILD PROCESS - Getting what you want from whom you want it in your childhood memory and efforts to rescript this memory.

(2) NURTURING PARENT PROCESS - Detaching from the situation you want to change.

(3) NURTURING PARENT PROCESS - Being able to decrease or remove an obstacle between you and the other person in your meditation.

Now let's tie all this together. As long as you fear the critical parent within you, you will not be able to get what you want from that "parent figure" or surrogates for him/her. Further difficulty in detaching or removing an obstacle indicates unresolved anger in you at that parent. You may have been unable to take responsibility for internalizing their message and acting out their script as your own.

This block may feel like it was imposed by another person. However, inability to develop the nurturing parent within you and to nurture yourself indicate this block still exists within you. It is not coming from outside sources, anymore.

The goal now is to identify this block. When you are able to do that, you will discover the major lesson you are here to learn and remove in this lifetime. That is a big motivator to do this work.

If you cannot resolve these difficulties on your own using exercises such as the ones I outline in this chapter, I urge you to seek the assistance of a licensed psychotherapist who can help you understand and resolve the karmic lessons you have brought into this lifetime to learn.

You can write or phone the Association for Past Life Research and Therapies. Ask for referral to a therapist in your area. Address and phone number are in the Bibliography at the end of the book.

NEEDS OF THE CHILD PROCESS
PRACTICE EXERCISE

1. How to Identify the Unmet Need of the Child Within You

   a. Think about a situation in your adult life that is bothering you.

   b. Close your eyes. Take several deep breaths. Relax.

   c. Accept the first memory from your childhood in this lifetime that pops into your mind spontaneously. Don't think about it. It will come to you.

   d. Describe this Childhood Memory:
      1) Where are you?
      2) What is happening?
      3) How old are you?
      4) Who is with you? Are you alone?
      5) How do you feel emotionally?

   e. Other questions to ask yourself?
      1) What do you want as that child?
      2) From whom do you want it?
      3) Write down the answers to one and two each time you do the Needs of the Child Process.

2. Rescripting the Childhod Memory

   Continue to be that child in your mind. Ask for and get what you want from the person you want it. Do it over and over as long as you want to. Open your eyes.

3. <u>NOTETAKING</u>

If you are able to get what you want from whom you want it when doing this meditative exercise, you have resolved the issue you are examining.

If you are unable to get what you want from whom you want it when doing this meditative exercise, the issue remains unresolved with that person.

Take time to write down what happened when you rescript this incident. Write down your thoughts and feelings!!

4. <u>HOMEWORK</u>

If you get what you want in this exercise, I suggest you continue to do this scene over and over on your own. The more you do it, the more it becomes part of you.

If you did not get what you wanted in in this exercise, the next step is to devise homework in the physical world to help you meet the unresolved need of the child within you.

EXAMPLES: Go on a fishing trip. If you wanted to go with your father and couldn't, ask an older male friend to go. Slide down a snowy slope on with a sled. Buy a kite. Run in a park. Buy yourself a balloon on the way home.

NEEDS OF THE CHILD PROCESS
WORKBOOK PAGES

EXAMPLE ONE:

What did you want as the child in this
memory?

From whom did you as the child want it?

Now close your eyes and try to get what
you want from whom you want it as the
child in this exercise. Write down
whether you are able to do that or not
and any other thoughts or feelings.

EXAMPLE TWO:

What did you want as the child in this
memory?

From whom did you want that?

Now close your eyes and try to get what
you want from whom you want it as the
child in this exercise. Write whether
you are able to do that or not and any
other thoughts and feelings.

EXAMPLE THREE:

What did you want as the child in this memory?

From whom did you as the child want that?

Now close your eyes and try to get what you want from whom you want it as the child in this exercise. Write whether you are able to to do that or not and any other thoughts and feelings.

IMPORTANT NOTE:
This is a good time to reach for your notebook/journal and write emotionally about whatever you are thinking and feeling. Write as long as you want to. When you feel done, then return to the next exercise in this WORKBOOK.

LOSS PROCESS

If you know someone who is grieving for
the death of a loved one or who has lost
a job or a valued possession, or whose
relationship has ended, Loss Process can
help them grieve.

The loss of anything or anyone is a death
or an ending, and it is natural to grieve.
Often all one needs is a sympathetic ear.
You may feel a grieving person needs more
or you may feel you should do more. However,
they may only need you to listen and be
supportive. Loss Process helps you become
a better listener.

The first thing to know is they need to
cry a lot. Tears are a healthy and important release. Let them cry. Just hand
them a kleenex box!

Some people grew up believing crying is
natural only for babies. If they put
themselves down for being a "cry baby,"
tell know crying is a natural part of
grieving for anyone of any age. If they
start to cry, don't tell them it's okay
to cry. Sit quietly until they stop.
Don't force them to talk. When they are
ready to talk, they will. Don't lecture.
Don't push. Hand them kleenex and listen.

The second thing to know is when they
start talking about their loss, it may
trigger grieving about earlier losses.

For example, let's say someone has just died. That person may have had previous illnesses. In encouraging the person to talk about a recent loss, do not hesitate to validate their need to talk about earlier losses regarding the same situation.

Eventually, they will feel they have talked enough about the recent past, but they have not yet finished grieving. If they are open to it, Needs of the Child may prove helpful to get in touch with earlier losses connected to the present.

Childhood losses that come up for them may seem "unimportant". Needs of the Child Process reveals the truth. The unconscious makes its own connections even if what it reveals is discounted.

Let them talk about the childhood loss that surfaces through Needs of the Child Process. If they did not get what they wanted in this incident, they may be unable to rescript it. They may also not be ready to do the homework. At the very least, Needs of the Child helps them identify what they need to work on later.

The bottom line of grieving is often anger, depression and sometimes guilt. It is natural to feel angry at the one who died, to be depressed about losing a job or valued object, to feel guilty they didn't "do more" to prevent a loss. They may have been unable to do more but believe "If I had only..." If so, try Guilt and Lay Every Thought Upon the Heart. If they blame someone else for events, try the Blame Process.

KARMA AND LOSS

Karmically, loss of a loved one requires physical and emotional closure. It is important that a person not deny emotions at a time of loss. Grieving is healthy. Metaphysically, completing one's grieving frees the departed's Soul to continue its karmic journey to the next incarnation.

There may be other things the individual wishes to explore, for example: "Have I known him/her in a past life?" If that arises, you can suggest they do a past life regression with a reputable regressionist to help them explore past life connection with the Soul that has left.

Finally, some people need to see a therapist when grieving, especially if they feel depressed about the loss. Even if one believes in reincarnation, death can be traumatic. Therapy helps overcome feelings of loss, depression and being overwhelmed by events.

LOSS PROCESS
PRACTICE EXERCISE

1. Current Loss

    a. When one is ready to talk, find out when and how he/she got the bad news. Ask him/her to start at the beginning and talk about it.

    b. Keep a box of kleenex handy. Let the person cry whenever and as long as he/she needs to.

c. Ask the person to describe what happened next?

d. If the loss is not over, ask the person to bring events up to the present or even to a future date (e.g. expected future death of a loved one, foreclosure on a house or anticipated job layoff.)

e. When he/she has described the loss from beginning to end, ask the person to close his/her eyes. Do a Thought Form on the emotionally powerful moment of loss. Encourage acting out emotionally against the Thought Form. It is healthy to ventilate emotional feelings.

f. The Thought Form may be black or red, signifying anger.

   EXAMPLE: Red box with a black bow. I want to smash it.

2. Previous Losses

a. When the person is ready to go to the next step, you might ask them to describe an earlier loss with the same person or situation.

   EXAMPLE: An earlier illness that was not fatal but did require hospitalization.

   EXAMPLE: Previous job layoffs when friends got fired.

1. Start at the moment the earlier bad news was received.

2. Ask the person describe the situation and his/her feelings.

3. Continue the story to its ending or bring it up to the present.

4. Don't interrupt. Be supportive. Urge him/her to tell you more until the person wants to stop.

5. Always keep the kleenex handy in case he/she needs to cry.

6. If he/she gets angry, encourage venting anger e.g. Thought Forms.

3. Earlier Losses - repeat as needed.

4. Childhood Losses

a. Ask the person to close his/her eyes. Do the Needs of the Child Process. Ask for the first loss of anything or anyone from childhood in this lifetime that spontaneously pops into his/her mind.

b. Have him/her open the eyes and tell you the whole story from beginning to end. What was the nature of the loss experienced in this incident?

1) It can be anything from a doll to a dog to a family member to moving from their childhood home and losing their friends.

2) Follow the questions in 1(d) of
Needs of the Child Process. Do
not interrupt. Let him/her talk.

c. The person may say they see no
connection between the childhood
loss and the current loss and
may discount the importance of
the childhood memory. Support
his/her talking about it anyway.
It may prove helpful to talk.

d. If he/she is open to it, do the
Needs of the Child Process. Does
he/she receive what he/she wants
from whom he/she wants it in this
childhood incident? If so, doing
this as homework can be positive.
Don't insist on it. A grieving person may not be ready for this.

5. <u>PAST LIFE REGRESSION</u>:
<u>FOLLOW-UP TO THE LOSS PROCESS</u>

People grieving for the death of a
loved one may want to do a past life
regression to find out whether they
knew the deceased in a past life, and
if so, when and what their past life
relationship was. This can help deal
with the loss now.

If you are looking for a reputable
past life therapist, contact the
Association for Past Life Research
and Therapies (APRT) which has members
throughout the United States and in
many foreign countries. Phone:
(714) 784-1570.

DEVELOPING THE NURTURING PARENT PROCESS

Ancient wisdom states one of the main purposes for relationships between people is for each to inspire the other towards greatness and harmony. We all have this innate spiritual potential within us. It is sometimes called the "Inner Christ" or "God Consciousness".

At the same time, we attract challenging situations and people into our lives to help us learn Karmic lessons and enhance our personal growth. We can learn lessons by conflict, crisis, pain and suffering, or through love, forgiveness and beauty. The choice is ours. We sometimes have to learn we have a choice.

A crucial step towards learning lessons through love rather than pain is to work through and detach from our internalized "critical parent" negatives and instead enhance the nurturing parent within us.

Spiritual consciousness reinforces doing things in relationships with others out of love and cooperation even when our lesson may be to express anger to someone we love. Metaphysically, anger and love are the same energy: one is negative, the other is positive. Some people find it difficult to understand this. Think of it this way. It takes time and practice to express anger to a loved one and to change negative energy (anger) to love. Learning to do this is the crux of Developing the Nurturing Parent Process.

NURTURING PARENT PROCESS has three parts:

PART I helps you detach from a negative
person or situation without denying your
anger or anxiety.

If it is difficult to complete Part I and
move on to Part II, do not push yourself.
You have not completed involvement with
the old negative situation. If you are
stuck in Part I and cannot change it, you
are still angry. Do Part I as long as you
need to. Repeat the Needs of the Child,
Circle/List Process and exercises from my
book, MEDITATIVE AND PAST LIFE JOURNAL,
to ventilate your negative feelings.

PART II helps you enhance new positives
and replace old negatives. When you have
worked through anger and are ready for
higher spiritual consciousness, Part II
feels relieving and uplifting.

PART III fosters Goodwill between you
and another human being by removing a
negative block within yourself. This
negative within you has prevented the
relationship from working. However, it
probably feels as if you are removing a
block between you and the other person.

If you want to know more about the Metaphysics of Goodwill, read Torkom Saraydarian, The Science of Becoming Oneself,
chapter 2. This book is available in New
Age bookstores.

DEVELOPING THE NURTURING PARENT PROCESS
PRACTICE EXERCISE

Part I. DETACHMENT FROM THE OLD NEGATIVE

a. Write a negative belief you want to change because it has blocked you in your relationship with somebody.

> EXAMPLE: I am afraid to ask someone for what I want because I will be rejected or criticized as selfish.

b. Detachment Exercise:
Close your eyes. In your mind be in a situation where you experienced this negative. Then, change the situation to solve the problem or improve things in some way. Next, go back to being in the old rut with the situation unchanged. Alternate back and forth several times until the second scene feels more comfortable than the first. Even a small change is just fine. This is what detachment feels like. Open your eyes.

c. Do not suppress your feelings. A small shift from one to two is perfectly acceptable. If you are unable to do this step, reread the previous page and try the things I suggested for anyone who cannot do Part I.

Part II. <u>POSITIVE REPLACEMENT OF AN OLD</u>
<u>NEGATIVE WITH A NEW POSITIVE</u>

a. Write down a new attitude or lesson you have just learned doing Part I.

b. Close your eyes. In your mind act out this new attitude or lesson in the specific situation you have been examining.

   EXAMPLE: Let's say you learned you never know if you can get what you want if you don't ask. So, in your mind you decide to try asking and see how it feels.

c. Next, do a Thought Form on the emotional feeling connected with your new attitude or action. Do what you want with that Thought Form over over in your mind as long as you want to.

d. The combination of the new attitude or belief and the new Thought Form, together, are exactly the formula I use in past life regressions. The combination repeated over and over reinforces the positive lesson.

e. My only caution is that whatever you got spontaneously you want to do with your Thought Form, repeat it unchanged. Repeating the same Thought Form powerfully reinforces positive change with your subconscious mind.

Part III. <u>INSPIRATION OF GOODWILL IN</u>
<u>ANOTHER PERSON</u>

   a. Do the Karma Drill to reinforce
      the benefits to you of the new
      positive belief or feeling.

   b. Close your eyes. Act out the new
      belief or attitude in the relation
      ship with the other person. Do it
      again and again until you feel an
      obstacle or block has been removed.

      EXAMPLE: You are expressing your
               real feelings about some-
               thing to the other person
               and the other person
               responds by expressing his/
               her real feelings to you.

   c. Open your eyes. Identify what block
      or obstacle has been removed
      between you and the other person.
      Write this down.

      EXAMPLE: You can express anger
               towards a loved one.
               He/she loves you anyway.

   d. Close your eyes. Do the following
      three things together:

      1) Say the words of your new belief
         or new attitude over and over.

      2) Use your Thought Form over and
         over in your mind.

      3) Experience the changed situation.

e. Rescripting
   The three steps I just itemized
   are the same combination I use in
   past life regression in what I call
   Rescripting. After you have gotten
   your new Affirmation and are doing
   what you want with your Thought
   Form, I have you experience the
   positive change in each incident
   in the past life and this lifetime
   as you return to the present. In
   the Nurturing Parent Process, you
   have the opportunity to experience
   how positive change is reinforced
   through the meditative state.

DEVELOPING THE NURTURING PARENT PROCESS
WORKBOOK PAGES

PART I. DETACHMENT FROM AN OLD NEGATIVE
IN A RELATIONSHIP

a. Describe a negative situation that
   has damaged your relationship.

b. Close your eyes. Experience this
   situation in your mind. Now, change
   it in some positive way. Then,
   experience it unchanged. Go back
   and forth until the change feels
   more comfortable than the original.
   Open your eyes.

PART II. POSITIVE REPLACEMENT

a. <u>Affirmation</u>: Write your lesson or new attitude from experiencing this changed situation. <u>Underline the key phrase in your Affirmation</u>.

b. <u>Thought Form</u>: Close your eyes. Repeat the underlined words of your Affirmation over and over. As you say them, notice how you <u>feel</u> about the change. Now, do a Thought Form. Do what you want with it. Open your eyes. Describe your Thought Form and what you did with it.

Part III. INSPIRATION OF GOODWILL TOWARDS
         THE OTHER PERSON IN A RELATIONSHIP

   a. Do the KARMA DRILL. List benefits,
      advantages or lessons to you of the
      improved situation. Write the list.
      Then, add one more (the stretch):

   b. Reinforcement of Change
      Close your eyes. Repeat the words
      of your Affirmation (underlined
      words in Step 2a). As you say that
      over and over in your mind,
      experience a change. Then describe
      what has changed:

c. <u>Removing the Block</u>
Describe the block or obstacle you
feel you have lessened or removed
between you and the other person in
this relationship. In reality this
block has diminished within you,
but it feels as if it was between
you and the other person.

d. <u>Reinforcing the New Positive</u>
Close your eyes. Experience the
following three things together.
Do them as homework often.

1) REPEAT YOUR AFFIRMATION - Write
the underlined words (step 2a):

2) Do what you were doing with your
THOUGHT FORM. Write step 2b:

3) Experience the CHANGED BEHAVIOR
(steps 3b and 3c).

Repeat the steps for several minutes. This is "Rescripting" as I outline it in PAST LIFE REGRESSION GUIDEBOOK.

Healing Parent-Child Relationships

This technique effectively reinforces with the subconscious mind the change you want to integrate into a relationship. Karmically, the most important obstacle or block you lessen or remove using this exercise is between you and one or both of your parents, your guardians or other parent surrogates.

When you do this exercise a second or third time, it is important to select the parent, guardian or parent figure with whom you have had the most difficult relationship in this lifetime. Do this exercise to help heal that relationship. It is important work.

KARMA AND THE NURTURING PARENT

Self-nurturing is what the Nurturing Parent Process is all about. To develop loving relationships with significant others, you have to learn to love and nurture yourself first.

Love is not a commodity that you acquire from the outside world the way you buy bread. It is a quality developed within you. As you become comfortable with it, you attract others who are comfortable loving and nurturing themselves.

The Metaphysical Law of Correspondences applies here. As above, so below. As within, so without.

Nurturing Parent Process teaches you to overcome that critical voice inside you that has told you for a long time you are "selfish" if you do or want something for yourself or have strong feelings about something important to you. ("Now, Mary! Let Sally play with your doll. Who cares if she breaks it? We'll just buy you another one. It's just a doll! Don't be so selfish with your toys!")

In reality, self-nurturing quiets the internalized voice that criticizes you as "selfish" or discounts you when you do what you want, express your own feelings and take care of your own needs.

You can't learn to express love to others until you have learned to love yourself.

So, Nurturing Parent Process like Needs
of the Child Process before it, helps you
learn self-love and then how to reach out
to others from this new, positive place.

Of all the exercises I have created for
PAST LIVES, PRESENT KARMA WORKBOOK, most
people say Nurturing Parent Process is
the most difficult to master. The reason
is the blocks that make so many relationships unloving, dysfunctional or
even abusive have been learned and internalized for many years. It is emotionally
painful to accept the reality that negative behavior one dislikes is now within,
and the only way to change the external
situation is to change oneself. That
is what makes Nurturing Parent the most
difficult exercise in the WORKBOOK.

Whenever someone gets stuck and resists
moving forward in Nurturing Parent Process, I suggest going back to Needs of
the Child Process. The inner child is
angry or hurt and needs to ventilate
feelings. Some childhood memory may be
trying to emerge. Needs of the Child is
a helpful way to ventilate and make it
easier to do Nurturing Parent Process.

There are 3 ego states within each of us.
The inner child needs to feel loved, to
play and to get its physical and emotional
needs met by the nurturing parent or it
sabotages the adult who is supposed to
take care of business (e.g. go to work).
When self-nurturing occurs, child's needs
are met and adult functions adequately.

Some people have a hard time distinguishing parent from adult. The parent is either
critical or nurturing, by definition. Its
interactions are with the child ego state.
By contrast, the adult takes care of business and is emotionally detached from
parent-child interactions. If you have a
critical parent ruling your mind and emotions and are not self-nurturing, you have
an unresolved problem from your childhood
relationship with your parents or guardians.
Seeing a therapist could prove helpful to
to resolve these issues.

When doing Nurturing Parent Process, the
block you lessened or removed may have
felt like it was between you and another
person, but it was within you. You cannot
change another person no matter how much
you would like to. Their willingness to
change is up to them.

The block you are removing within you is
actually the core of what you have been
working on throughout this WORKBOOK. In
different ways, it comes up over and over.

I said in the Introduction, there are 3
lessons around which karmic issues form:
tolerance (including self-love and forgiveness); self-responsibility (including
owning one's anger); and self-esteem
(which depends on mastery of the first 2).
These issues are often at the root of
relationship problems, too.

To make learning karmic lessons easier, I
added a new exercise called "Creating
Self-Love and Self-Esteem Process".

CREATING SELF-LOVE AND SELF-ESTEEM PROCESS

Overcoming such problems as break-ups of personal relationships teaches us consciously what we as Souls already know: we are here to learn to give individual meaning to our lives. Confronting relationship challenges refocuses attention on self-discovery and personal growth.

The most difficult barrier for most people to overcome is to learn self-love, self-nurturing and self-esteem. So, answers to questions in four exercises in PAST LIVES, PRESENT KARMA WORKBOOK give solid clues to removing blocks and achieving goals.

In my experience, there are four major behavior patterns that damage our ability to love ourselves and develop self-esteem:

a. suppression or discounting of our feelings including anger and hurt

b. giving up or lowering personal standards and values in an effort to receive approval from others

c. setting unachievable perfectionist goals for ourselves or attempting to become the rescuer of other people in order to avoid living our own lives

d. being unable to achieve self-forgiveness, a form of self-punishment that leads us to feel undeserving and to create undeservingness in our lives.

Through relationships, we project onto
significant others the fantasy of ful-
fillment of our unmet needs and wants
which we may feel powerless to fulfill.
We may fantasize that self-mastery will
lead the significant other to abandon
and not love us. Overcoming such fears
empowers us to meet our own needs. Self-
mastery is the path to learning to love
ourselves and create self-worth.

It is a common pattern that guilt, fear
and anger at loved ones have roots in
past life relationships. We carry these
unresolved feelings into our present life
relationships, not to be stymied by them,
but to learn from them this time.

Unfortunately, in the pain of the moment,
it is easy to lose sight of why we chose
these relationships in this lifetime. So,
we must gain mastery in the present. Then
it is wise to discover past life connections. Following this sequence makes
resolution of past life issues deeper and
more permanent.

SELF-LOVE AND SELF-ESTEEM
WORKBOOK PAGES

1. Find your answers to the following
   questions and summarize them here.
   (They are keys to understanding what
   blocks you need to remove to love
   and nurture yourself.)

   a. Guilt Process - page 65 (Step 4):

   b. Lay Every Thought Upon the Heart
      Process - page 79 (Step 3):

c. Manifestation Process - page 93
   (Step 5):

d. Nurturing Parent Process
   page 133   (Step 3c):

2. Now, review Needs of the Child Process
   (page 117-118). If you were <u>unable</u> to
   get what you want from whom you want
   it in this exercise, write here what
   you were <u>unable</u> to get and from whom
   you couldn't get that:

   a.

   b.

   c.

3. Now, ask the following questions (one at a time). Close your eyes. Accept the first words that pop into your mind. Open your eyes. Write them down. Continue until you are done:

   a. WHAT DO I <u>NEED OR WANT</u> THAT I DO NOT NOW HAVE?

   b. WHAT DO I FEAR <u>LOSING</u> IF I GET WHAT I WANT AND DESERVE?

c. WHAT DO I FEAR <u>GETTING</u> IF I RECEIVE
   WHAT I WANT AND DESERVE?

d. WHAT <u>INTERNALIZED MESSAGE</u> DO I NEED
   <u>TO GET RID OF</u> IN ORDER TO MANIFEST
   WHAT I WANT AND DESERVE?

e. WHAT MESSAGE DO I WANT TO
   SUBSTITUTE THAT WILL HELP ME
      LOVE AND FORGIVE MYSELF?

4. Write down any other thoughts or
   feelings you are having now. Take
   your time.

5. <u>Self-Love and Self-Esteem Summary</u>

Repeat Lay Every Thought Upon the Heart and Manifestation Processes to create what you want and need.

Do Needs of the Child Process to let "the child" in you play and to ventilate negative feelings or anxiety.

Do Nurturing Parent Process every time an issue comes up between you and another person in a relationship.

Continue to write down your thoughts and feelings each time you feel the need to express yourself. Use the exercises in my book, MEDITATIVE AND PAST LIFE JOURNAL, to help you express your feelings and get help from your Higher Self and spirit guides.

As I am fond of saying: "These exercises work, if you do."

ADMIRATION AND GRATITUDE PROCESSES

The person you love or the person in the relationship you are trying to heal does not have to be told you are doing this work. You are, in reality, working on yourself. The other person will respond to the extent he/she is ready to receive the love you are conveying.

The Admiration and Gratitude Processes are intended to release your negativity and help you convert your negative emotions to love. To the extent you succeed in making this transformative step, you will feel lighter, calmer and more positive. Heaviness and negative speech are tip-offs to your resistance to change.

It is interesting to note that admiration and gratitude are higher forms of love energy. They lack emotional intensity but can be felt emotionally, nevertheless. As you work through anger, love is released. This transformation is basic to Metaphysics. Admiration and Gratitude are simply more spiritual expressions of love.

If you want to find out more about the Metaphysics of Admiration, read Torkom Saraydarian, The Flame of Beauty, Culture, Love, Joy (pages 124-125). Gratitude is discussed in Torkom Saraydarian, Cosmos in Man (pages 63-70). Both books are available in New Age bookstores.

ADMIRATION PROCESS
PRACTICE EXERCISE

1. Old Negative

   Identify any anger/greed/jealousy/
   envy/unhappiness/frustration in your
   present life. Think about what you
   do not have and want. Think about who
   has what you wish you had.

2. New Positive

   a. Find something you admire about
      the person who has what you lack.
      Observe the beauty in that person
      or the thing or ability they have.

      EXAMPLE: They are always well
               groomed and have a good
               sense of color matching.

   b. Close your eyes. Admire that
      character trait, thing or ability
      in your mind for several minutes
      until you feel a subtle release
      of admiration towards the person
      or thing you admire. (This is a
      gentle love energy.)

   c. Do a Thought Form on your feeling
      of admiration. (This is beauty and
      love you are releasing.)

      EXAMPLE: Perhaps, you really like
               a dress or suit you have
               seen this person wear.
               Admire it in your mind.

ADMIRATION PROCESS
WORKBOOK PAGES

1. Old Negative

   Describe an anger or other negative
   situation in this life you want to
   change. Indicate what you lack and
   wish you had. Think of a person who
   has what you don't have.

2. New Positive

   a. Describe a character trait, object
      or ability you admire the person
      for having. Describe its beauty.

b. Close your eyes. Admire that trait physical object or ability. Feel admiration released towards that.

c. Do a Thought Form. Describe it.

d. Do Manifestation Process on getting trait, object or ability.

GRATITUDE PROCESS
PRACTICE EXERCISE

1. State a criticism you have thought or
   voiced to or about another person,
   perhaps something that is damaging
   the relationship with him or her.

2. Find something this person has said or
   done that warrants your gratitude.
   Find something to say, anything that
   feels real for you.

3. Express your gratitude out loud to
   him/her as if you were talking to that
   person now. Say it over and over aloud
   until you can say it naturally without
   giggling or feeling like you memorized
   the words. Practice Step 3 looking
   yourself in the eye in a mirror until
   you are comfortable saying it

4. Close your eyes. Do a Thought Form on
   your feeling of gratitude. Do what you
   want with your Thought Form.

5. Repeat your statement of gratitude and
   do what you want with the Thought Form
   until you _feel_ a positive release of
   love towards the other person. Repeat
   this as homework.

6. Write down thoughts and feelings about
   your relationship with the other person and anything else you want to say.

GRATITUDE PROCESS
WORKBOOK PAGES

1. Write down a criticism you have voiced
   or thought about a person you know.

2. Write something about which you feel
   gratitude towards the person you have
   been criticizing. Make it simple.

   EXAMPLE: "I feel gratitude you put
                 trash in the trash basket."

   Now, fill in your own sentence:

   "I feel gratitude that ...

3. Repeat Step two in front of a mirror
   out loud over and over as if you were
   talking to the other person. Do not
   drop your gaze. Do it until you don't
   giggle with emabrrassment. Relax your
   muscles. Notice your resistance. Practice every day until you can talk to
   the person instead of the mirror.

4. Close your eyes. Do a Thought Form. Do
   what you want with it over and over.
   Open your eyes. Write a description.

5. Homework: Repeat the statement of gratitude and what you do with your Thought Form as long as you want to.

6. Practice your statement of gratitude in front of a mirror until you are ready to say it to the person.

7. Write down your thoughts and feelings.

KARMA AND TRANSFORMATION

It is basic Metaphysics: the energy of resistance is also the energy of transformation. The effort needed to maintain an old negative belief system and repress negative emotions can become the power to resolve a problem when you are ready. The crucial factor in changing negative to positive is emotional readiness.

Positive change happens when you confront the truth you had been resisting and invest your energy in resolving problems. This transforms negative Karma into positive Karma. It is the reason we as Souls reincarnate lifetime after lifetime.

As you identify and resolve Karmic lessons, you open the way to experiencing your past lives through regression and discovering your Spiritual Purpose for incarnating this lifetime. Both are rewards for working on yourself now.

There are additional way to find out about your Soul decisions regarding Karma and Spiritual Purpose. They are:
1. past life regression
2. the meditative and past life journal
3. the natal astrological chart.

I have written books and created spoken audio tapes volumes on these subjects. If you want to do more personal growth work, you might want to buy them from your local bookstore or from me by mail order. Here are the titles and descriptions:

MY BOOKS:
PAST LIFE REGRESSION GUIDEBOOK
2nd edition - 4th printing - 128 pages
bibliography

Easy to follow, step-by-step explanation
of meditative techniques. Sample past
life regression. Detailed instruction
on how to past life regressions.

Chapter about my spontaneous past life
memories as a Comanche Indian that began
my career as a past life regresionist.

New case-study chapter: "How Our Past
Lives Influence Us Now"

ISBN 1-879005-11-5   Retail $10

MEDITATIVE AND PAST LIFE JOURNAL

64 pages   illus. bibliography

Meditative techniques teaching you
how to dialogue with your Higher Self
and Spirit Guides, problem-solve in
the present, predict the future,
explore other dimensions, discover
your own past life memories.

ISBN 1-879005-02-6 Retail $10

FINDING YOUR LIFE'S PURPOSE THROUGH ASTROLOGY WORKBOOK

Co-authored with astrologer, Mark Vito

64 pages - many illus. and examples

Techniques for analyzing your birth chart and understanding what karmic lessons and spiritual purpose you brought into this lifetime.

Step-by-step explanation for beginners and advanced students of astrology.

ISBN i-879005-03-4   Retail $10

<u>MY SPOKEN AUDIO TAPE VOLUMES</u>:

PAST LIFE REGRESSION

8 spoken audio tapes paralleling
PAST LIFE REGRESSION GUIDEBOOK
taped during classes and workshops
including a full length past life
regression.

Retail $29.95

MEDITATIVE AND PAST LIFE JOURNAL

Four spoken audio tapes detailing the
four parts of the methods outlined in
MEDITATIVE AND PAST LIFE JOURNAL.

Retail $15.00

FINDING YOUR LIFE'S PURPOSE THROUGH ASTROLOGY

8 spoken audio tapes of classes based on the FINDING YOUR LIFE'S PURPOSE THROUGH ASTROLOGY WORKBOOK.

Retail $29.95

PAST LIVES, PRESENT KARMA

8 spoken audio tapes from classes based on PAST LIVES, PRESENT KARMA WORKBOOK.

Retail $29.95

PSYCHIC PHENOMENA OF REINCARNATION

8 spoken audio tapes on such topics as: karma, Soul choices, role of the Higher Self, Souls meeting those they have known before, families reincarnating together, psychic protections, negative entities, walk-ins and being from other universes.

Retail $29.95

LIFE, DEATH AND REINCARNATION

8 spoken audio tapes on such subjects as how to know if we have known someone in a past life, Soul mates, Deja vu, Soul evolution, karmic relationships, do animals have Souls, differences among Souls, spirits and ghosts.

Retail $29.95

You can buy these books and spoken audio volumes in New Age bookstores. If your local bookseller does not carry them, ask them to order them for you from one of my distributors:

Baker and Taylor Books
Moving Books Inc.
New Leaf Distributing Co.

You can also order my books and audio tapes by mail order from me directly:

Bettye B. Binder
Reincarnation Books/Tapes
P.O. Box 7781
Culver City, CA 90233-7781

Add $2.00 for each book and each audio tape volume you order by mail to cover shipping costs.

California residents must also add 8 $\frac{1}{4}$ % state sales tax.

I wish you positive transformation now!!

BIBLIOGRAPHY

Bailey, Alice A. A Treatise on the Seven Rays, Vol. I (Lucius Publications, 1936). This book has now been subdivided as follows:
Esoteric Psychology I and II;
Esoteric Astrology III;
Esoteric Healing IV;
Rays and Initiation V.

Capacchione, Lucia. THE CREATIVE JOURNAL: THE ART OF FINDING YOURSELF (Chicago, Illinois: The Swallow Press, 1979).

Joy, W. Brugh. Joy's Ways, A Map for the Transformation Journey (Los Angele CA: J.P. Tarcher, 1979). Chapters 1 - 9.

Juriaanse, Aart. Bridges (Pretoria, So. Africa, Bridges Trust, c. 1934).

Saraydarian, Torkom. Cosmos in Man (Agoura, CA: The Aquarian Educational Group, 1973), Chapter VI, "The Rays and the Human Soul," pp. 73 - 79 and Chapter VII, "Ray Meditation Techniques," pp. 84 - 95.

_____. The Hierarchy and The Plan.

_____. The Science of Becoming Oneself.

_____. Symphony of the Zodiac.

_____. The Flame of Beauty, Culture, Love, Joy.

_____. The Science of Meditation.

Sutphen, Dick and Trenna. The Master of
          Life Manual (Scottsdale, AZ:
          Valley of the Sun Publishing
          Co., 1980). pp. 7 - 49.

Young, Robert and Loy and Capacchione,
          Lucia. Reincarnation Hand-
          book, Techniques of Past
          Life Regression (Los Angeles,
          CA: Reincarnation Research
          and Education Foundation,
          Inc. 1980). Out of print.

For past life therapist referrals:
Association for Past Life Research
          and Therapies (APRT)
P.O. Box 20151, Riverside. CA 92516.
Phone: (714) 784-1570.